THE LAST RAIL

ODYSSEY

Like Theodore Judah, my father was a visionary engineer. Like A.J. Russell, he was a pioneering photographer. My father designed the camera lens that flew into space on the first U.S. weather satellite. That Tiros satellite is displayed in the Smithsonian Air and Space Museum. This book is dedicated to my father and all who envision new achievements on the land or in space. —D.B.

To my wife Deborah and our daughters Allison and Caitlin —B.F.

Copyright © 1996 Trudy Corporation, 353 Main Avenue, Norwalk, CT 06851, and the Smithsonian Institution, Washington, DC 20560

Soundprints is a division of Trudy Corporation, Norwalk, Connecticut.

Book design: Alleycat Design Inc. New York, NY

First Edition
10 9   8   7   6   5   4   2   1
Printed in Hong Kong

Library of Congress Cataloging-in-Publication Data

Bailer, Darice.
    The last rail : the building of the first transcontinental railroad / by Darice Bailer ; illustrated by Bill Farnsworth.
        p.   cm.

    Summary: While on a field trip to the National Museum of American History, ten-year-old Lucy imagines herself as Andrew Russell, taking a picture of the joining of the Central and Union Pacific Railroads at Promontory Summit, Utah, in 1869.

    ISBN 1-56899-362-5 (hardcover) . — ISBN 1-56899-363-3 (pbk.)
    [1. Pacific railroads—Fiction. 2. Railroads—History—Fiction.
3. School field trips—Fiction.] I. Farnsworth, Bill, Ill.
II. Title.
PZ7.B1447Las   1996
[Fic] —dc20
                                                                96-15036
                                                                   CIP
                                                                   AC

THE LAST RAIL

Written by Darice Bailer • Illustrated by Bill Farnsworth

Soundprints
Where Children Discover...

"Hold still!" Lucy pleads, fumbling with her camera lens. She and her friends, Kevin, Tomas, and Emma, are visiting Railroad Hall at the National Museum of American History.

The long, green steam locomotive parked along the museum wall is posing quite nicely. But Tomas isn't. He's doing jumping jacks. Kevin holds up two fingers behind Emma's head. Emma, meanwhile, is sticking out her tongue.

"Cut that out!" Lucy cries, exasperated. She's supposed to take pictures for the student newspaper. She wants to do her best. But her friends aren't making it very easy.

Suddenly the children hear the sound of a steam locomotive screeching to an imaginary halt—*Pssss!*

Startled by the recording, Lucy drops her camera.

Her friends dash off and Tomas accidentally kicks Lucy's camera across the brown brick floor.

"Oh no!" Lucy groans. "What if the camera broke?" She stoops down to pick it up and comes face-to-face with a large black-and-white sketch inside a glass case. The drawing shows dozens of men crowded around two old railroad locomotives. Standing at Promontory Summit, Utah, on May 10, 1869, they're celebrating the completion of the first Transcontinental Railroad. At this spot, according to information in the exhibit case, the Central Pacific Railroad crews building east from Sacramento, California, met with the Union Pacific crews coming west from Omaha, Nebraska. The two railroads had set down 1,776 miles of new track across the western frontier.

"This is a sketch of a very famous photograph by Andrew J. Russell!" Lucy recalls. "I've seen it in my American history book. I can't get three people to stand still, let alone this big group! And not one person is sticking out his tongue! How did Mr. Russell ever do it?"

ucy picks up her camera to photograph the case and suddenly sees an entirely different picture before her. She finds herself peering from beneath a black cloth covering the back of an old-fashioned wooden camera. The camera rests on a tripod, alongside a wooden wagon.

Hey, who put this cloth over my head? Lucy wonders, as she throws it off and looks around her. *And who are all these men?*

All of a sudden, Lucy takes a big gulp. "I'm not back at the museum any longer *looking* at the sketch," Lucy says to herself. "I'm *taking* the actual photograph!"

How did I ever get here? Lucy wonders. But she doesn't have time to figure it out. Someone in the crowd of people is waving to her and asking, "Mr. Russell! How much longer until you're ready to take the picture?"

Lucy begins to protest. "See here! I'm not A. J. Russell. I'm just a ten-year-old girl!"

Then, as Lucy glances down, what does she see? Baggy black trousers and brown stiff boots! Lucy may think she's just a little girl, but she's wearing a man's clothes!

A gentleman doffs his hat to her. "Good day, Mr. Russell! I'm so glad you'll be recording this event! Imagine. The last spike being laid today. We've conquered the wilderness! Opened up the continent! Why, we've opened up the world!"

Lucy grins. It might be fun to play along with this. She lowers her voice to sound like a man. "Why yes, we have," Lucy replies in her best grown-up voice. "And this photograph will be displayed in books and museums for years to come." Lucy's quite sure of that!

"This is the funniest camera!" Lucy says to herself.

Luckily, she knows a great deal about the history of photography. She giggles to herself as she removes the glass plate from inside a wooden chest resting on the ground beside her. In the 1800's, photographers didn't have film. They had to mix some chemicals and pour them over a glass plate. The chemicals helped turn the glass plate into a negative that could be used to print a picture on paper.

She sees that the wagon beside her contains more photographic materials, so she climbs up to peek inside. *This must be A.J. Russell's traveling darkroom,* she thinks while she hunts for the equipment she'll need.

Outside the wagon, she overhears two people talking.

"Poor Theodore Judah," one man says. "When he dreamed of building a railroad across the continent, he wanted to make travel easier through the West. It's too bad he died so young—in 1863."

"The same year this railroad was started," says the other.

How sad, Lucy thinks to herself. *Theodore Judah never lived to see his dream come true.*

14

Lucy jumps down from the wagon. She's curious about all the workers gathered around her. She sees two Chinese men with long pigtails standing nearby. She approaches them and introduces herself as Andrew Russell.

"How did you ever build a railroad through those mountains?" she asks.

"It was very hard," says one of the men, who introduces himself as Yang Li. "It sometimes took all day to chip away just eight inches with our picks and shovels. It took us three years to lay 100 miles of track through the Sierras."

Lucy shakes her head. She's about to ask Yang Li and his friend Long Ho why they didn't use a bulldozer or digger, but she catches herself just in time. There were no gasoline-powered machines back then! No wonder it took the workers so long.

Suddenly, Lucy notices Yang's right hand. She can't stop staring at it. He's missing his fingers!

"The black powder got them," Yang says quietly.

Lucy listens, spellbound, as Yang tells his story. "We were building the railroad along the cliffs above the American River Canyon. I drilled small holes and set blasting powder inside. Then, I would light the powder and run to get clear of the blast. The rock on the mountain was so hard that the powder sometimes exploded out of the hole like a cannon."

Yang Li sighs. "One time, it caught my hand before I could get away."

"The mountains were tough, but remember those winters, Yang?" Long Ho asks. "It was the winters that nearly killed us! The one at Donner Pass was incredible. You've never seen so much snow. It would pile forty feet high in a storm!"

"Forty feet!" Lucy repeats in disbelief. *That's even taller than my house,* she thinks. *And, imagine the snow days. School would be closed for weeks!*

Long Ho interrupts Lucy's thoughts. He points out how dangerous the snow could be to the workers. "The snow was so powdery that we'd sink to our shoulders," Long Ho said. "And, there were many snowslides that buried people alive. We had to dig them out."

A group of workers from the Union Pacific join Lucy and the others. They brag jokingly to the Central Pacific workers that their route west from Omaha, Nebraska, was more difficult than the course east from California.

"But we had the Sierra mountains to blast through," Yang Li argues back, holding up his hand.

"Well, we had the Lakota-Sioux and Cheyenne Indians on the Great Plains of Nebraska," says a worker named Patrick from the Union Pacific, pointing east.

Lucy remembers reading about the Indian raid at Plum Creek. Understandably, the Native Americans didn't like the Iron Horse. The railroad's hunters had killed thousands of buffalo for hides and pushed the Lakota-Sioux and Cheyenne off their homeland.

"Yes," Lucy says, summoning her grown-up voice again. "How sad it must be for the Indians to watch us celebrate this railroad. It can't be much of a celebration for them."

Lucy wants to hear more but she'd better get back to work. What would happen if the photograph didn't get taken?

As Lucy dips the glass plate in a flat metal pan filled with more chemicals, she overhears another group of workers talking to a reporter.

"In the end, the Central Pacific and the Union Pacific were twenty-five miles apart and racing to the finish. Whichever railroad laid the most track would earn the most money," said a Central Pacific worker named Miguel.

"Even though our Union Pacific tracks met up with the Central Pacific tracks, our bosses were too stubborn to quit. Our grading crews passed each other by over one hundred miles," laughed Patrick from the Union Pacific.

Lucy finishes preparing for the photograph just as everyone begins to assemble for the driving of the last railroad spike. She looks out over the large group gathered for the ceremony, all having played an important part in the building of this extraordinary railroad.

They left their families to work in this wilderness and open it up to people everywhere. The pioneers who traveled out west were just like the astronauts exploring outer space. To the immigrants, the West was a new world, untouched except for animals and Indians. Now, people could travel from the east coast to the west coast in two weeks. New towns would be built. The East could now have access to the products they needed from the West. Trade would open, not only in this country, but with Asia and Europe. What an incredible feat.

"On my next trip," says the Central Pacific engineer, holding up his bottle of champagne, "I'll bring silver, lead, and copper from these mountains to the manufacturing companies back east."

"And on *my* next trip," says the Union Pacific engineer, "I'll bring settlers, tools, and supplies to build new houses and farm this land!"

Lucy lifts up the glass plate and watches the ceremonies begin. *Jupiter* of the Central Pacific is on the left. It faces *119* of the Union Pacific on the right. Chinese workers set down two iron rails between the two locomotives.

Mr. Leland Stanford, one of the owners of the Central Pacific Railroad, holds up a shiny golden spike. It is engraved with a special message. "'May God continue the unity of our country as this railroad unites the two great oceans of the world,'" Mr. Stanford says aloud, reading the inscription to the crowd.

That golden spike and another are gently tapped into a railroad tie and then removed for safekeeping. Mr. Stanford tries to hammer in the last of four iron spikes and misses. *Mr. Stanford's workers are much better at building railroads than he is!* Lucy thinks, chuckling to herself. The workers howl, too. "He missed it!" the crowd yells with glee.

Attached to Mr. Stanford's silver hammer is a wire. It leads to a telegraph resting on a nearby table. Although Mr. Stanford missed the spike, a telegraph operator sends the message to the rest of the country. *Done,* the operator taps. The news flashes across the country along the telegraph wires strung beside the new Transcontinental Railroad.

The two locomotives gently move forward to touch.

Lucy's glass plate is set. She inserts it into the camera. Get ready everybody!" she yells. "I've got to take the photograph quickly!"

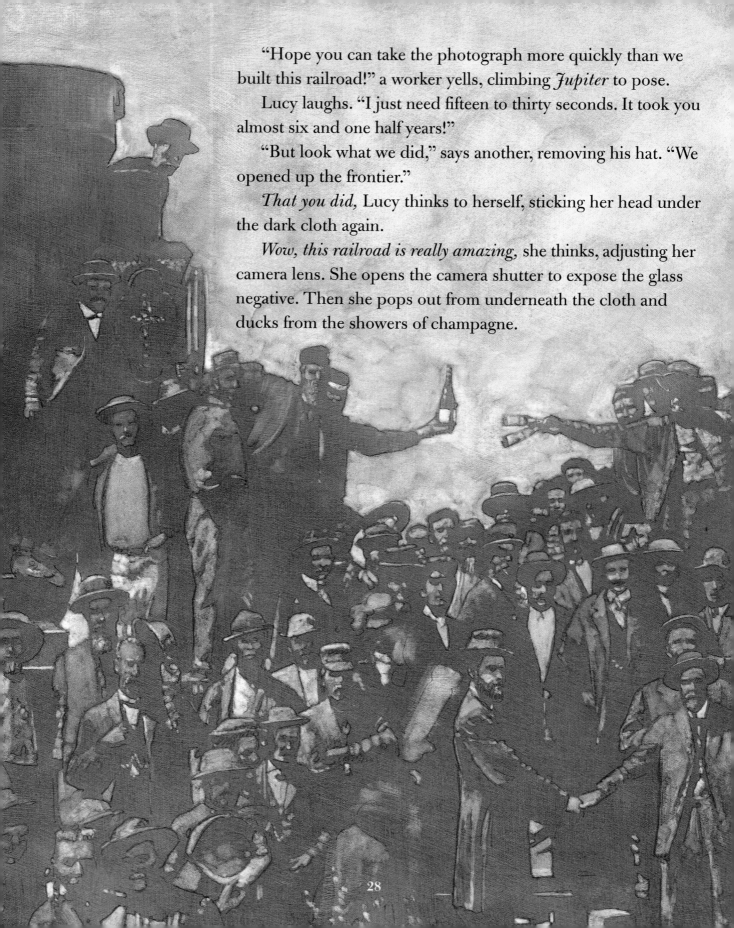

"Hope you can take the photograph more quickly than we built this railroad!" a worker yells, climbing *Jupiter* to pose.

Lucy laughs. "I just need fifteen to thirty seconds. It took you almost six and one half years!"

"But look what we did," says another, removing his hat. "We opened up the frontier."

That you did, Lucy thinks to herself, sticking her head under the dark cloth again.

Wow, this railroad is really amazing, she thinks, adjusting her camera lens. She opens the camera shutter to expose the glass negative. Then she pops out from underneath the cloth and ducks from the showers of champagne.